I0625934

ASCENSION

Awakening to All Things Beautiful

by

Tyra Smith

Printed in the United States of America

ISBN- 978-1-960853-70-7

Liberation's Publishing House
Columbus - Mississippi

ASCENSION

Awakening to All Things Beautiful

TABLE OF CONTENTS

To The True and Living God, Jesus Christ, His Son and My Lord and Savior and My Help The Precious Holy Spirit.

LET ME BEGIN BY SAYING...

I have grown so much spiritually and have done so much personal development since writing my first book. My healing journey has really sped up. Sometimes, we think we have healed from our past, only to learn that it was just one layer and that there are multiple layers of healing. I was told that healing is like an onion with lots of layers, and that was not far from the truth at all. When you take a raw onion and start cutting it, the tears begin to roll down. With every cut made, there is a special pain that comes with those tears. The burning sensation is so bitter, and that, to me, is exactly what it is like to go through the layers of healing from pain—years later, you find yourself reopening the wounds.

This reopening gets you to the junk that we refused to deal with when it first happened to us. We refused to do the work, pushed it down, put a pretty rug over it, and called it a day. With life and with the healing process, take it one day at a time. I read in a book that just doing 1% better than you did yesterday can do a lot for the future you. Please understand that not all of your decisions in life were bad. You did what you thought and felt was best for you at that time. Sometimes, we can get so stuck on thinking about all the wrong decisions we believe we made. We don't

Tyra Smith 1

understand that the past is the past and was a part of the planned journey of our lives. Our perception of ourselves, shaped by our past pains and traumas, makes a big difference.

I used to look at my past and wonder, *What did I do to deserve this? Why is my life not right? Why didn't anyone love me?* There was a part in my first book where I asked God why He gave me the parents I had, why I was not lovable, and simply—why? As I was writing *Behind the Scenes of a Calling,* I remember hearing the word perception.

My perception was not any good. It made me blame the people who hurt me and even God. When I started to understand that I could have a different outlook on my life and past trauma, I knew that God was offering me a new way to view my life. Yes, the past trauma hurt terribly, but why? Why did it hurt me so badly? Was it because I made it all about me?

Maybe I should have been thinking that the person who hurt me only did so because it was all they knew. It was what they had learned, and deep down, they were hurting too. What if all they had ever known was hurt? They didn't even realize that their subconscious was bringing up what was hidden deep inside them.

When do we get to a point where enough is enough and start asking God (the universe) why we behave the way we do? Why do we experience hurt the way we do? I have learned that we only mimic what we have learned or what we have experienced. We learn from those closest to us and from the things we hear and see as we grow up. It becomes instilled in us.

In Philippians 2:12, it says, *Work out your own soul salvation with fear and trembling.* Why do you think the Bible says this? Well, let's talk about it.

As we go through life and collect pain, hurt, and trauma, it all weighs down our soul. And it happens at a time when our soul should be evolving. How can it truly evolve if we are carrying all this baggage? We are not working through these emotions that we have.

Let me say this: It's okay not to be okay.

It's okay to have a bad day. It's okay to feel hurt. Your feelings matter, and they are valid. But don't think for one moment that you can just ask God for healing and not have to work through it and walk through it. Some of the things that hurt us are obvious, because we think about them from time to time.

When we see, hear, smell, or taste something, it triggers a memory of past hurts. Just seeing an image of a person who hurt you can instantly take you back in time to that moment—it's unreal.

I remember having one of those moments. One day, I was driving on the highway when a song played on the radio. Suddenly, I had an instant flashback of the guy I wrote about in my first book—Freight Master. He worked with me at a freight company. When that flashback came, the feelings and tears came with it.

Those feelings and tears helped me realize that I had not processed those emotions.

Years ago, I was told that, in time, all wounds heal. True, but we have to understand that there's a catch to that. The catch is that we must acknowledge that we are hurt, that it's okay to feel what we feel, and that we cannot push it down or bury it. If we don't process it, we will find ourselves almost twenty years later writing a book, telling the whole world our life story and secrets.

I believe that whatever area we struggle with the hardest is usually where we can find our calling and purpose.

I struggled with love—and that, my friend, was a matter of the heart. I had to endure a hard road of hurt and pain so that God could teach me how to heal myself. Afterward, I could help others heal and teach them how to rid their souls of the toxic things we tend to pick up along the way.

I know that if I struggled so hard in this area, there are so many others struggling with the same thing. They are being terrorized by their past and feel stuck, not knowing how to move forward and truly be happy from the inside out.

This is how God works—from the inside out.

You can't change the outside and think that the inside doesn't need to be addressed. It works in that very order: inside out, not outside in.

What is in us flows out and around us.

If you're wondering why your life is such a mess, baby, let me be the first to tell you: *You are the mess on the inside—cut and raw.*

That is how it was given to me.

We should always be doing some kind of personal development so we can strive to be 1% better every day.
I love doing shadow work—let me explain.

Shadow work is where we bring or allow hidden emotions to come to the light. Those situations that we don't want to think about or allow to surface.

How many of you know that when you expose darkness, light comes in, and the darkness must flee?

This is what we should be doing—allowing God to bring up certain emotions, feelings, and situations that we have not addressed and keep covering up.

Tyra Smith 5

Awakening to All Things Beautiful

LEARNING TO LOVE SELFLESSLY

As I gazed into his eyes, I knew deep down that maybe I should not do another round of this. I had been so good at staying in my lane and making sure I kept a clear path from all men. But there was something about this one that took me to a special kind of fairyland, with hopes and dreams of him being the one. His caramel-smooth skin and eyes that I couldn't resist. His smile drew me in so deeply that I couldn't say no to getting to know him.

By the end of the conversation and him asking me for my number, my knees had already buckled twice. I honestly don't know how that was possible.

Freight Master had stolen a part of me with just one conversation and a smile. I knew at that point this was one of two things: either he knew the magic that he carried, or I was just weak as hell in the knees at the one-minute mark. Either way, he had me at hello and a smile. He didn't even have to say anything to draw me in. As he rode off on his forklift, all I could do was smile big and stay in La La Land for the rest of the day.

This thing started off really well. He knew what time I would come to work, and he would just be waiting for me to hit that dock. Deep down inside, I knew I loved coming to work just for the attention that the men gave me. Don't judge me. I had deep-rooted daddy problems that I wasn't aware of at the time. Looking back on my childhood, my mom gave me everything she could. I believe a lot of it was to make up for my dad not being in my life—her not knowing at the time that there was nothing anyone could do to fill the void in a little girl's heart from wanting her dad. Her being a daddy's girl herself, that void, that dark hole, just grew and grew over the years.

Look, I get that some people can just wipe that pain off and keep going without a problem. On the other hand, there are people like me who don't understand the deep impact that this can have on them. Fatherlessness has a huge effect on a little girl's life, even affecting them into adulthood. I felt like I was trying everything—church, God, praying, fasting, and even being celibate for some years. It was like no matter what I did, I kept failing in the men department and disappointing myself and God.

As Freight Master and I kept talking and texting, we got closer, and finally, he ended up inviting me over to his house to watch movies and have dinner. I know what you're thinking: *Oh, she's going to give him some.* Actually, I didn't. I was surprisingly good when I went over there. I can't say the same for him. Yes, he tried me, but I was proud when I left his house. I had not allowed myself to go there with him— not yet, at least.

When I tell you that I am not sure how I ended up falling head over heels for this man, but I did. I had no idea that the relationship was going to break me in ways I had never imagined.

As we kept going in the relationship, I started noticing weird things. I would call, and he would be over at an ex-girlfriend's house washing her car. Other times, she would bring her clothes over to his house, and he would wash them. Yeah, I would say those were big red flags. Now, ask me if I walked away. Yup, you guessed it right. My crazy self stayed and kept going. But not without expressing to him how what he was doing was really hurting me.

Now, this is the part where I feel like I was learning a valuable lesson. I was learning how to express myself in ways that I had not learned up to that point.

Side Note: I was a people pleaser, and I would hold all my feelings in and not express them at all. Did you know that when you hold on to your feelings and emotions, it makes your soul toxic? You start to gain weight in your hips, and sometimes you can experience really bad hip pain. Holding emotions in can also block your expression, and your expression is connected to your creativity—which can stop you from being the creator that God has made you to be.

We are meant to create because we come from the Creator, made in His image and likeness. But me, being a people pleaser, I never wanted to say things that would hurt or offend anyone. I didn't want anyone to leave. I felt that it stemmed from the trauma I had experienced with my father—the hurt and pain of feeling like I wasn't doing anything right or that I had done something wrong to make him want to leave me behind.

The way I see it now is that Spirit (God) is always offering us a new perception and outlook on life. It is up to us to take it or leave it. If we take what is being offered, it opens the door to change and understanding—that we all have different perceptions because of what we have learned, seen, and experienced in this thing called life.

Here I am, offering you a new perception of your pain and hurt. As I dig deeper into my understanding of my pain and truth, I say *truth* because both books tell the truth of my feelings and emotions. They both tell how my past affected me then and how I now perceive my past from a new perspective.

Telling my truth back then was always so hard for me to express, but now that I've been doing it, it's getting easier. Back then, it was hard because I always cared about what people thought of me and what they thought in general.
I've learned that whatever a person's perception of me is, it's none of my business. That is for them to work out for themselves.

Me thinking that telling him how I felt about what he was doing was going to cause him to change was the start of a new change. This was the first time I was willing to express my emotions to anyone. He was the first, and I thought that expressing myself would be taken into consideration. I thought he would consider my feelings and think twice about his actions.

Weeks passed by after expressing myself, and everything seemed great. We were getting closer than ever—or so I thought. Then I found out that he was still paying her phone bill. Ask me how I found out. Sometimes, if you just sit back, people end up telling on themselves—for real. And that was exactly what he did.

How I see it is that God will never let you stay blind to someone doing you harm or hurt—especially when it comes to matters of the heart.

Nonetheless, I called myself so in love. I was just in La La Land, passing up all the red flags. I guess deep down, I just wanted this endless love that I had dreamed of and always thought about. And I guess I was willing to take the risk of my heart being played with just to have a taste of love—or at least, what I *thought* was love.

When it came to love, I was willing to risk it all for love's sake—the strongest emotion one can experience, and one that I know *God is*. He is love.

To be honest, back then, I don't think I could tell the difference between fantasy, illusion, and reality when it came to love.

Tyra Smith 11

WHAT IS SPIRITUAL

So, let's talk about spirituality. What does it mean to be spiritual? Some people think that going to church is spiritual, but that is not the case. A major part of being spiritual is truly working on the unseen things—your hurt, insecurities, and deeply rooted issues that others cannot see. The more these things are unpacked, the more your soul can evolve and expand. God flows from the inside out, not the outside in. That means if your physical world is a mess, then you have mess inside of you that needs to be addressed. This is where personal development comes in.

In religion, people often like to blame the devil for things when, oftentimes, it is actually God trying to push us toward something new and different. Other times, it's their own damn self—self-sabotaging. The very thing we claim to want, we fear the possibility of succeeding in, or we fear failure. That is one question I think we should all ask ourselves before uttering the words, *The devil is trying to do something to me. Am I self-sabotaging myself?*

Our thoughts lead to feelings, our feelings lead to action, and action equals results. Just think about this for a moment: If we pay attention to the thoughts that come to us, we can teach our brain which thoughts to keep and which ones to dismiss. After a while, you'll realize that a thought you just had wasn't a good one, so don't allow it to stay. You can change your belief system by changing what you think repetitively. Did you even know that your belief system is made up of what you think over and over again? Be careful about what you allow yourself to keep thinking.

This is one of the reasons why the Bible says, *Be transformed by the renewing of your mind.* Just by the way it's worded, we have to know that this is an ongoing transformation, not just a one-time thing.

Nevertheless, there I was, on the floor, tears rolling down my face as I stared at what I had believed to be my worst enemy. I was engulfed in betrayal, lies, being unloved, feeling unworthy of love, misplaced trust, hurt, and the pain of secrets from the past—without realizing that my worst enemy was myself and the perception I had allowed myself to believe for so many years. Let me be real. I believed that perception my whole life. *It's me. I am the reason no one loves me.*

What was wrong with me? Was I not good enough? Am I not worthy of the love that I dreamed of? And if I was truly worthy, how would I even know it to be true? I was so used to not feeling loved that I wasn't sure if I would recognize it when I saw or felt it. I was so busy trying to give what I *thought* was my version of love that I didn't understand that I had to first learn to love myself. But how? How would I even start this journey of loving myself? What did that even mean or look like?

My perception was that everyone I encountered treated me badly—so I treated myself badly too. How would I begin this road to self-care and self-love? Then I started to think: *If I don't love myself, how can I truly say that I love God?* If He abides in me, and I am supposed to be made in His image, how could I claim to love Him when I couldn't even love myself? I felt even more lost than when this journey began. Taking this step to write a book was the start of my healing journey, but it also opened up so many questions in my mind. While I was stuck in these questions of life and self-discovery, my whole world—the only one I knew—was being destroyed. In the midst of losing everything in the physical, the *old me* was thinking, *That damn devil is not going to take me down. I'm going to fight to the very end before I let him steal what I believe is mine!*

I didn't understand then that God is a God of order, and in order for Him to build, He first has to tear down old foundations. No construction builder is going to build on top of an existing building—they first bring in everything needed for demolition. Everything must go. The whole foundation has to be destroyed.

Everything I believed to be true was, in fact, *not* true. Not only were things being destroyed in the physical, but my belief systems were being dismantled. When we stop trying to fast and pray just to touch the surface of Him, and instead start going deeper—truly digging beneath the surface—He reveals exactly what we ask for in depth.

All I can say is, I felt the shaking and the destruction in both the spiritual and physical worlds. Seeing and feeling both was terrifying, but I trusted the process.

I had moments when I didn't know what to think or do about what was happening. All I could do was keep learning, growing, and working on myself. Many of us know there are things in our lives that need to be broken and destroyed, yet we find it easier to act as if they don't exist. But ignoring them doesn't help us be true to ourselves.

There are times when I have to remind myself to put myself first—to stay courageously true to myself no matter what or who is standing in front of me. To be true to oneself is to be true to God.

When talking about perception, it's important to learn how to shift your perspective when trying to understand something. I do this often when interacting with people—it's a powerful tool to have. Understanding that *your* perception isn't the only one that matters is key. Proverbs 4:7 says: *Wisdom is the principal thing; therefore, get wisdom: and with all thy getting get understanding.*

When Jesus walked the earth, He never made sinners feel bad about themselves. He didn't point fingers. Instead, He had a deep understanding of the people of God. He didn't come to shame anyone—He came to show us a better way to treat one another, with understanding and compassion.

What if I told you that the pain and hurt we experience could be lessons to help us shift our perspective? When we feel wronged by someone, why do we make it about *us* instead of thinking about the individual doing the hurting? Maybe they have been hurt so much that hurting others is all they know. Maybe this is a generational wound—something passed down from their parents.

I say this because I used to take everything personally. I didn't realize that the way people treated me wasn't *about me*—it was about *them* and what they had been taught. Understanding this led me to empathy—not sympathy, but *empathy*. If you're not careful, sympathy can lead to manipulation. I started to realize how much I was operating in sympathy—feeling bad for people and letting that pull me into people-pleasing. But learning to use empathy instead helped me step away from doing things out of guilt and start doing them because I *chose* to.

In the midst of the shaking in both realms, I kept telling myself, *Everything will be okay. I will make it through this.* But still, the inevitable was happening. I didn't know how bills would be paid, and it looked like I wouldn't have a place to live.

All I had was a mustard seed of faith—and *man*, that was it. If you know what I'm talking about, you *know*.

One of the scariest parts was that I could see what was happening in both realms. I had never experienced it this way before. On one hand, it was the most amazing sight. But on the other hand, I was asking God, *Why?*

I had taken such a leap of faith by writing my first book. I knew my intentions were in the right place—I wrote about my pain so people would know they weren't alone.

UNEXPECTED ANSWERS

As I started preparing for my kids and me to leave our home, I began selling and giving away the very things I had worked hard for. I had been volunteering at the local food bank every Thursday for the past month, helping them load up cars with food for those in need. Every Thursday, volunteers would show up to help, and at the end of the day, all the volunteers would get their cars in line and receive food as well. We took turns doing this until every volunteer had food in their car. These were carloads of food, not just for the volunteers but also for the people who came through needing assistance.

I would drive home, unload the food, and then share the overflow with my neighborhood. If this wasn't biblical, I don't know what was—He was filling the barn to overflow so much that I didn't have room enough to store it. So, I gave out the excess. After filling my house, I would first go to two older women who lived on the corner of my street and let them pick what they needed. Then, I would move on to others who might need it. If we don't help the elderly, who will?

I also set aside some food for my neighbor because they had kids who liked the same things as mine. As I stocked up for my house, I also saved some for their children. My neighbors were genuinely nice and sweet. I was the prime example of the biblical text: *Love thy neighbor as thyself.* Taking care of the elderly—how much more biblical could one get?

Every time I walked into my kitchen, I saw so much overflow that I had to believe blessings were here, and that it couldn't be possible that we would have to leave our home. My kids were my biggest support through it all. At every step of getting closer to leaving our home, they reassured me that God would take care of us and provide. How sweet and innocent they were! They had the faith I was lacking, and yet, I was supposed to be the one telling them that everything would be okay and that we would make it—somehow, some way.

There wasn't a night that passed without my fear growing stronger, afraid of what would come next after we had to leave. I cried many nights while my kids were either asleep or at school. Having to sell everything and give everything away made this situation a reality that I dreaded so much. But seeing my kids come home with their bright faces, not having a care in the world because they carried a whole bag of mustard seeds compared to my one, gave me hope. As each day passed, reality set in more and more—*What was I going to do? Where were we going to go?*

I started getting angry with myself. For the first time in my life, I had invested in something I wholeheartedly believed in—writing a book. Yet, it wasn't going anywhere or having the impact I believed it could have. My heart was hurting so badly. I didn't understand. I was in awe of what was happening to me. I had no one in my corner supporting me, no one to lean on or help me. I didn't know it then, but I know now that I was continuously dying to myself. Forget daily—this felt like an *hourly* process. The Bible says that we die daily, but for me, it felt like every hour, especially since I was only days away from having to leave my home.

Three days before we had to leave, the tears stopped. They just ceased. In that moment, I suddenly knew that everything was going to be okay and that we would be taken care of.

I had moved most of my things out of the apartment and was finally at peace with whatever was going to happen. My plan was to go to a hotel and figure out our next move. Everything had been so stressful, and so much was happening that I just wanted to sleep well and regroup. Let me say—during this entire time in my apartment, I couldn't find a job to save my life. I just couldn't understand why. I applied for so many positions, it wasn't even funny.

I had authored a book, yet I was at a complete loss as to why everything was happening this way. The only thing I could say to God was, *Okay, you're done destroying—let's get to rebuilding so I don't have to leave my home. Alright, God, let's go.* But at every turn, destruction was still happening. I'd turn another corner, and there'd be a moment of rest. Then, I'd turn another—and BAM! Damn it! *You're not done yet, God? How much do You need to tear down?* My goodness, this must be one of those *Everything Must Go* sales I love to go to— except now, *I* was the one going out of business and being foreclosed on.

On my last day in the apartment, the property manager came to do a final inspection. I handed her the key, and she turned around and gave it back. She told me she could give me one more day to figure out where my kids and I were going to go. As we spoke, my next-door neighbor was also there, buying some of the things I had for sale.

After the manager left, my kids and I sat on the couch in silence—not knowing what to think. We were relieved to have one more night, but the question still remained: *Where are we going to go tomorrow?* At least this saved us one night in a hotel, because I knew that was where we would eventually have to go until we figured things out.

My neighbor ended up buying quite a few things from me—all the TVs, some tables, and my washer and dryer. As he was leaving, I mentioned my book, and he bought a copy. I really appreciated his support. He and his girlfriend may have needed the things they bought, but I *definitely* needed to sell them for the money. We talked—not just about my book, but about a lot of spiritual things as well.

Later that night, as my kids and I were eating dinner, we heard a knock at the door. When I opened it, I was surprised to see my next-door neighbor again. He said, *I have an apartment in North Georgia that I keep for my mom, but she's no longer staying there. If you and your kids need a place to stay for a little while to figure things out, you're welcome to use it. Just let me know if you need to.*

I was so surprised that I couldn't respond right away. I told him I'd let him know later that evening if we needed it. That night, as I drove to the bank to deposit money, I knew deep down that I needed to take this offer—we still had no place to go. But I was hesitant. *What's his angle?* I didn't know my neighbors that well, so I wasn't sure if I should accept. But I knew deep down that I needed to.

The next morning, after packing the rest of our things into the car, my neighbor texted me the address. I put it into the GPS—*an hour away.* He had left ahead of us, I assumed to get the place ready. My kids and I made a few stops before getting on the highway. They were so excited that God had made a way for us.

They kept saying, *See, Mom? We told you God was going to take care of us! We just had to believe!* I don't think I had ever seen their faces so bright-eyed and full of joy.

As we got closer, we realized this wasn't just a hill—it was a *mountain.* When we arrived, the apartment was beautiful, with an amazing view. My neighbor gave me the key and told us to make ourselves comfortable. Then, he left.

I tried to stay in the moment and embrace the present. My mind naturally wanted to race ahead: *What happens when we have to leave here? Where will we go next? What's next, God?*

I realized that if I focused too much on the 10th step, I would miss the step that was right in front of me. I had to be careful not to trip over the very rock that *God* had placed in my path.

THE MOUNTAIN

This mountain was very familiar to me. *Where had I seen this before?* I started asking myself. This mountain reminded me of the land of Moriah, the mountain where Abraham's faith was confirmed by God. When I tell you that I jumped up and down with so much joy, amazed that I was on this mountain—so many spiritual things were happening to me up there. I knew that every step I took had been ordained by the Most High. I could feel it. When I slept, I could feel the angels around me. They were doing something to the top of my head. I wasn't really sure what was going on, but I knew it wasn't bad. It didn't hurt or anything. The feeling of warm vibrations came in like clockwork.

Within the first week of us being on the mountain and exploring, we found a beach 15 to 20 minutes away. We would get up at 6 a.m. and be at the beach by 7 or 8 a.m., and I would just worship, pray, and meditate. Every moment spent there, I always asked God, *How much better can this get?* Taking in the sight and the smell, watching bald eagles fly high—it was just the most beautiful and peaceful place to be.

We would go to this beach at least once or twice a week. My kids loved it there. Just thinking about the time we spent there brings me happy thoughts and smiles. Talk about complete peace and solitude. Trust me when I say that when you have that incredible feeling of complete peace, it *will* be tested sometimes. Allow your peace to be unmovable. You must remain tuned in and tapped in because it *will* be tested. I think my time in the mountains really shaped me for the journey that I didn't even know I was about to embark on. I really took advantage of the peace that gave me some understanding. I didn't have a worry in the world—I was floating on a cloud.

Not only did my kids and I go to the beach, but we also found a park nearby where I could walk while my kids played. But they didn't want to leave my side. So, as I walked, they walked. We looked around, took in the scene of nature, and rested on a bench here and there when they got a little tired. Sometimes, I would leave them there and continue my walk and talk with God.

Every time I went to that park, or any park for that matter, I would talk, pray, and laugh with God. I didn't care what people thought about me walking and talking to myself—if only they knew that we are never alone.

Even though I knew we couldn't stay in this apartment forever, I did look for places to live while I was there. I even tried getting an apartment in the same complex, but they didn't have anything available. I knew that was God telling me, *You can't stay on this mountain.* That wasn't a part of my purpose. He definitely let me know that I couldn't stay in the secret place forever—He needed me out so He could use me to touch the lives of others. I had work to do. So, I quickly got the idea of staying in the secret place out of my mind. Being in the mountains was for me to rest and recover after that big battle I had just gone through. So, I rested in the presence of the Most High.

My kids and I started a journey there of trying to make better choices about what we were putting into our bodies. If we were on this spiritual mountain and journey, I knew that my God is a God of truth. And knowing that, I also knew that He wasn't just going to change one part of my life and leave the other part in shambles.

This is a God who finishes whatever work He starts—no matter how long it takes. That, I know to be true of this amazing and most wonderful God that I serve. I really don't think we truly understand just how big God is, or how just and complete the Most High is.

This is a God of full circle, of completeness and oneness with all. I spent so much time searching for Him on the outside and didn't fully understand that there was no need to search—because He abides in me. The Most High, living through me, having a human experience. And I, through Him, having a God experience. Learning how to truly live is learning how to die—die to the different perceptions and conditionings we have been taught.

I was taught that we had to invite God in. But how would we invite something in that already lives in us? The Bible says, *Ye are gods and are created in His image.*

Looking back at my life, I was truly lost. And I had to learn that it's okay to be lost—because that only means that you *will* be found. I also started to understand that all the meditation, the walks in the park, and going to the lake were all ways I was connecting to the true essence of God within me. I learned so much during my time on the mountain. That's where the real work of working on me began. I gained an understanding of what spirituality truly is. And it wasn't found in going to a four-walled building, asking the Holy Spirit to *come into me* or *fill the room.* It was about understanding that God has always been there, whether we ask Him to be or not.

How can we truly say that God won't invade us unless we invite Him in—when He was our very first breath when we were born into this world? That was a planned invasion from the very first breath. Some of these realizations came to me a little later, but at that point in my life, I was learning that it is very important to work on personal growth. Being on that mountain truly blew my mind—all the things that were happening to me spiritually. Some things I felt, and some I dreamed. And knowing that when we dream, we are interacting with the spiritual world, it all became even more clear to me.

The time I spent there was truly amazing. Just sitting here, writing this, takes me back to how absolutely special that time was. The gratefulness, the joy, the abundance of love, the gratitude I send to God. While there, I couldn't even think about where we were going to go afterward. And to be honest, I wished I could have stayed there. But I was only supposed to be there for a season.

My kids and I stayed in the mountains for about a month. The day I got the phone call that we had four days to leave, my heart dropped.

Awakening to All Things Beautiful

GOD IS A GOD

But one thing I can say—God allowed me to see beyond the veil of what was happening. I definitely expressed to my old neighbor how much I appreciated him for letting my kids and me stay there as long as we did. I was truly grateful, and I knew that I wasn't going to be there long. Even though, deep down, I had no clue what to do next, I trusted the process of the God that I served. I started to pack up, pray, and look for somewhere for my kids and me to go.

I cried a few nights and prayed, and on the third day, I wiped my tears, looked up, and told God, "I trust You; show me where to go."

We ended up going to a shelter. When I got there, I went to the window and told them my situation. The man told me that they didn't have any beds available and asked me to sit in the lobby for a minute. As I waited, I sat in silence and told God, "I know You are making a way, and I know You didn't lead me here just for them to tell me they have nothing for us."

As I continued to talk to God, my kids and I sat waiting—just knowing that the man at the window would find us something.

From afar, I heard the man call me over to the window, and he said, "Ma'am, we have a family room that we are

Tyra Smith 31

getting ready for you and your family. I will call you back in a few minutes to get more information from you."

I sighed in relief, smiled, and thanked the Almighty God for making it possible.

See, my lesson from this was: if you can't be grateful for the small things—like simply having a place to sleep, no matter where it is—how can you be trusted to be grateful for bigger things? Your response to different situations is very important, no matter what you are facing.

I was so grateful and thankful that we at least had somewhere to be for the time being. Again, I wasn't thinking about the exit date but instead remaining in the present with gratitude.

But I also found myself wondering, "God, why am I at this particular shelter?"

Now that I was tuned in and tapped into the Spirit, I asked, "Why am I here?"

We have to begin to understand the importance of asking questions—and not just any questions, but the right ones. The universe hears all, so when we ask the right questions, we receive the answers meant for us. Digging deep within myself to find the right question about why I was there was important. While I was there, I continued doing the things I did in the mountains—praying, meditating, and going on my journeys to the lake as often as I could.

One day, as my kids and I were walking to lunch in the shelter, I noticed a chapel and often wondered why its doors were never open for people to go in and pray. Even though I understood that God is not found within four walls, I still questioned it.

So, I went on a mission to find out how I could get into that room. I finally figured out that all I had to do was ask the security guard to open the door for me if I wanted to go in. So, I started going into the chapel—praying, playing gospel music, and singing praises unto God.

I didn't realize that as I sang, my voice carried into the lobby until one day, a couple of people saw me coming out of the chapel and asked,

"Hey, are you the one that's always in there singing gospel songs?"

I said, "Yes, I didn't realize my singing could be heard in the lobby. I'll try to keep it down."

They laughed and said, "No, that's the reason I started sitting out here—to listen to whoever is in there singing."

They told me they didn't want me to stop.

I even caught the security guard standing by the chapel door, listening to me sing when I came out one day.

That's when God spoke to me and said, "Did you think I filled you up with all this light and wouldn't send you somewhere that needed a light to shine?"

"Omg, okay." I said. "God, use me however You need to."

See, when we go through our toughest times, we have no clue why we are in the place that we are in. Just like we never know *who* we may be entertaining—*we could be entertaining angels unaware.* Every person I encountered at that shelter, whether they were there for me or I was there for them, was a moment of encouragement and empowerment.

A shelter is a place of transition—leaving the old and stepping into the new. There are so many people stuck in that transition point who have lost all hope. Why would I think that, after leaving the mountains filled up with Spirit and overflowing, I shouldn't go into the trenches to help restore hope and encouragement to the people God sent me there for?

There are so many of us who slip through the cracks of society and are forgotten about. But while I was there, it gave me so much hope—knowing that even though we, as humans, forget about those who are lost in this world, God never forgets about them.

He sends people who aren't afraid to go into these dark places to restore light to the ones He chooses for us to deliver it to. I was a willing vessel—even though I didn't quite understand everything at that moment, I knew that my being there was bigger than me. We need to understand that our purpose on this earth is not just about us.

The challenges we face are not always about us. Sometimes, it's about the people we encounter along the way. I try to remind myself that it's bigger than me.

As I looked for a place, I just wasn't finding anything at all. At first, I didn't understand why. Why could I not find anything? I had the money. It just wasn't making sense to me at all. Then I heard God say, "Expand the search." Deep down, I knew what God was saying, but I wanted to live in a certain area. I was like, "Ummm no, God, I want to go over here in this area."

One part of me could just hear God saying, "Yeah, okay. You go ahead and run yourself tired. Let me know when you're done, and I'll tell you where to find what you're looking for. Just hit me up when you're tired enough."

Laugh out loud. All I could do was laugh and say, "Okay."

Eventually, I did get damn tired—almost to the point of no return. You know how sometimes God will let things happen to get you to move? Well, yeah. Let me tell you how this all went down. God had pointed me in the direction of moving out of the state of Georgia, and *boy* did I rebut against that. I didn't want to leave Georgia.

This was the place where I had found my spirituality. I had truly grown so much in God and elevated spiritually. Even though a lot happened here, this was the place where I was released into the unknown and learned to trust God.

Georgia held a special place in my heart—I had experienced success, heartache, growth, love, new connections, connections that needed to be broken, and healing.

Living in Georgia was my first time living outside of my birthplace, and I had been there for 11 years. I searched high and low to find a way to stay there.

CREATING WITH THE CREATOR

Since my mom had moved away, we talked more, and our relationship got better over time. In November, I decided to go and surprise her for Thanksgiving. For some reason, once I knew that I was going to take this trip, I decided to go with the flow and look at some apartments and houses while I was there.

But to be honest, I really didn't want to move there. I had lived away from my family for so long that I liked the distance between us. Moving to this place would mean being closer to family—within reach.

I don't say this to imply that I dislike my family, but when I was living in St. Louis, there was so much chaos and confusion. If you have read my first book, then you know exactly what I'm talking about.

I found comfort in being alone—away from my family. But deep down, somewhere in the pit of me, I *did* want to have somewhat of a relationship with them. So, when I went to visit my mom, I scheduled some appointments to look at houses and apartments. I stayed at her house for about three days over Thanksgiving.

The first day of searching was no good. There was nothing. Everything I looked at just wasn't it. After that first day, I went back to my mom's house and got online to see if

I could find something else to view while I was there. On the second day, it was the same thing. Nothing. I was lost for words. I wasn't understanding why. But I kept riding around, looking, and still found nothing.

So, I decided to go to a bar and grill and take my sorrows out on a glass of wine. As I sat at the bar in so much confusion, I kept looking at rental apps, trying to stay hopeful. I was determined not to leave until I found something. With only one day left before I had to leave, I began to cry and asked God, "Okay, where am I not looking?" And as I sat there, *drowning my pain in a glass of wine*, I opened up the app one more time.

And when I did, I saw a house. It didn't look bad, but I wasn't really interested in that particular style of home. But I sent a notification of interest anyway—just to see what would happen. As I sat there, talking to a friend on the phone—crying, drinking my sorrows away, and ordering another round of chardonnay—I heard my phone beep, signaling an incoming call. The caller hung up before I could answer. So, I got off the phone with my friend and called the number back.

A woman picked up and asked, "Did someone call this number? My name is Tyra."

I said, "Yes, I did. I sent an inquiry about a house you have for rent."

She responded, "Well, would you like to come by and see it? Do you know how far you are from the house?"

And I kindly said, "Ma'am, I'm not from here, and right now, I'm at a local bar, pouring my sorrows into a glass of wine."

She laughed so hard—which was not the response I was expecting.

But I was being very honest.

I'm sure she could probably hear in my voice that I wasn't joking. We made arrangements to meet at the house later that day. She probably felt I needed the recuperation before I came. *Laugh out loud.*

As I pulled up that evening at this house—a house I wasn't very fond of from the pictures—I brought all my paperwork and identification documents to show who I was. A married couple pulled up at the same time. We introduced ourselves, and I toured the house. Then we went down to the basement—which I hadn't even realized the house had. By this point, I knew if they offered me the house, I needed to take it—because honestly, I was tired. And I knew God knew I was tired too.

But let me tell you about this couple... The moment I shook their hands, there was a strong connection. After the tour, they offered me the house. I felt led to tell them everything—from my injury on the job to being homeless and not having a place to live. They looked at each other, then looked at me, and said,

"Well, Tyra, we really appreciate your honesty. We can feel the energy—there's a strong connection—and we would like to help you get into this house."

Let me tell you real quick—by the time this house came, I was damn near broke. If I wasn't already.

So, I told them the only thing I had at that moment was the deposit.

They told me, "Let's meet up tomorrow. You can sign the lease, pay the deposit, and we'll talk about the rest then."

When I tell you God always comes through, I mean it. We need to be co-creating with the universe—which is still God. Remember, the Bible says He goes by many names. Being able to co-create what we're asking for—while taking action steps—is the key to manifesting the life we want. You actually have to do the work. We can be on our knees all day—asking, wishing, and hoping—but if you're not willing to take action, you might as well be a sitting duck.

We have to remember that our God is a creator. And if we are made in the image of God, that means we too are creators. The Bible says, "If you seek, you will find. If you knock, the door will be opened unto you."

If the Bible says "Ye are gods", then how do we tap into that God essence and power?

How do we operate at our highest potential?

What steps do we need to take?

After leaving the couple, all I could do was cry and feel so grateful. My kids and I were on our way to having a home. To be honest, we were ready to go back to Georgia and pack up. But we still had one more step before we could call this house ours. I still had to meet up with them the next day, pay the deposit, and sign the lease. But I knew in my heart that this house was already ours.

We have to understand—if we're not finding what we're looking for in the perimeter of our choosing, then we are being called to expand our search. We must be willing to trust God and take a leap of faith into the unknown. And that, my friend, is where God meets us—in the unknown. Taking action on faith requires risk. We must be willing to leap toward what we want—knowing that God will catch us before we hit the ground. Just because it looks like nothing is happening, that's when we have to dig deeper and trust. Because it is already there—it's just manifesting into the physical at the appointed time. And when it does—it blows your mind.

If you don't envision what you want, how will you ever receive it? We are visionaries. If you think for one minute that we are not called to have visions of our future, then this book may not be for you. This book is meant to help expand your mind and deepen your understanding of God.

Awakening to All Things Beautiful

SHARING THE GLORY

Starting my new life in a new place, I hoped that at some point God would bring me a job or some source of income. Yeah, I had written a book, but I didn't know how to market it in order to produce sales. So, I put my hands to work at a shelter not far from my house—going in and helping them serve food. My kids and I loved doing this.

It was strangers who truly helped us when we were in need and homeless, so we thought, "What better way to give back than to help others the way we were helped?"

After five months of being in our new house, I landed a job. Before I get into this part, let me tell you—I had never really thought about a job in this way before. But I knew one thing for sure—I didn't just end up there by chance. I believe God strategically placed me there for a reason.

So, here we go.

I ended up getting hired to work at a prison. Yeah, I know. "Why, Tyra? Why?" That was the thought in my head. "Why, God, am I going into this place?" But I knew deep in my heart that God sent me there. Why *wouldn't* God send me into a place like that?

God's people are everywhere—and a lot of them are in dark places. Just because the people there were locked up for crimes they committed, it didn't mean that the people of light weren't supposed to go into those dark places and let the light of God shine. When you really think about it, God is light surrounded by darkness. At least, that's part of what the Bible says.

So, why are we, as humans, not operating at a God-like capacity—tapping into His power for the purpose we were sent here for?

As I went through training to become a correctional officer, we were taught many things. One of the biggest lessons was the difference between sympathy and empathy. That's where I truly learned the difference between the two. If we think for one minute that God won't use different jobs to teach us different things, we're only fooling ourselves.

He uses everything as a tool to teach us lessons. I also learned that this job would be what I made it. It could be hard or difficult—depending on my mindset. They taught us ways to protect ourselves—because let's be real, this job is and was dangerous for anyone walking into this career.

This job takes focus, empathy, and respect. The more I showed up for training, the more I kept asking God, "Are You sure about this?"

And God kept saying, "Yes."

But one thing He told me was that this wouldn't be a career for me—that I would only be there for a season.

I started pressing in more—meditating, praying, and seeking God's guidance. If this was what I was walking into, I wanted to make sure I was prepared spiritually.

Every morning, on the way to training, I would pray, listen to meditations, and ask God to guide me, protect me, and—most importantly—use me to impact the people He needed me to reach.

After about a month and a half of training, it was time for me to run my own dorm. Yes, I said dorms. These men were not in cells—most dorms held about 123 to 140 men with only one correctional officer. Yeah, let that ratio sink in for a minute.

Now, let me say this—I did not have proper field training before they let me loose on my own. During field training, I saw so many officers come into the dorms with terrible attitudes. Some of them were straight-up bullies. You could tell some of them had been picked on in school—because now, they were taking it out on the inmates.

If I haven't mentioned it yet, this was an all-men's facility. Yeah, I know. Shake my head. If you've read my first book, you already know why I'm shaking my head.

When I started, so many women were getting arrested—caught sleeping with the inmates. Did you know that if a female officer is caught sleeping with an inmate, the state can file rape charges against her?

She can go to prison for rape.

Yes—facts.

And once in prison, everyone becomes state property. So, the more I kept showing up for work, the more I saw. Some of my trainers were amazing. Others... well, let me leave that part alone. *Laugh out loud.*

One thing about inmates—they know BS when they see it. And sometimes, they could smell it before it even walked in the door.

One thing God had me understand before I walked into this place was that they were all people. They belonged to God, and no matter what crimes they committed, I still needed to treat them as such.

A big part of me knew deep down that being there was a test. This was training ground for me. I learned a lot while working there.

After my training, I had one last thing to do—pass the final test. Once I passed, they would release me into my position as a correctional officer. Usually, after passing, they still put you with another officer for a while to help you adjust to the daily tasks.

But not me.

The night I passed my test, they threw me into a dorm alone. And to be honest, I didn't understand why they did that. It was my first time in a dorm by myself. My heart was pounding. I was nervous as hell. I didn't know what to expect. And they put me in a dorm full of young guys—called the Education Dorm—because most of them were enrolled in school. By the time I arrived for my night shift, they were all back in the dorm.

When a new officer enters a dorm, it's test time for the inmates. They want to see what they can get away with. Manipulation is a highly practiced skill set there. They know exactly what they're doing. Some would straight up ask what rules we actually enforced—because with 1 officer to 130 inmates, you can't enforce everything. The advice given to me was:

"Pick the rules that matter most to you—and enforce those." And that's exactly what I did.

God gave me so much empathy for these men—stuck in the system. The hurt and abuse I witnessed was beyond anything I had ever seen. But favor followed me. The higher-ups began sending new hires for me to train. They also noticed something different about me.

Supervisors kept asking,

"How do you get these inmates to listen?"

"How did you build rapport with them so fast?"

The truth?

I used prayer, meditation, and the power of God to shift the atmosphere.

Because we are atmosphere changers.

We have the power to shift any room we walk into.

And that's exactly what I did.

Awakening to All Things Beautiful

BEING FEARLESS

Let me tell you about one guy in the dorm I took over. Many of the inmates claimed that he worshipped the devil because of some of the things he did when the lights went out. By this time, I had moved to day shifts, so I would walk into the dorm around 5:50 AM. Every morning when I arrived, he was always the only one awake, sitting quietly in the corner by his bunk. He didn't talk much, but he always smiled when I walked in. I had to walk up and down each aisle to count the bodies in the beds. When I passed him, he would nod his head and give a slight smile—and I would do the same.

The inmates would always ask me, "Why aren't you scared of him?" They thought I should be because of the things he supposedly did at night. I always told them, "I have no reason to be afraid."

Even though the inmates told me stories about him, I had never personally witnessed anything they described.
I never treated him any differently than the rest. I never felt bad energy from him. I could sense when one of them was playing mind games, but with him, I never picked up on anything negative. I was respected in every dorm I walked into—and I give thanks to the Most High for that.

One day when I got to work, my coworkers told me that one of the female officers had been beaten with a broom by an inmate. She was badly injured. Anytime I trained a new officer—which I was assigned to do many times—I made sure to teach them one thing above all:

The way you enter that dorm door will determine how the inmates treat you. I also explained that it's best not to come in rude and disrespectful. You want to build rapport, not come in hungry for power—acting like you can't wait to enforce authority.

If you do, you won't be respected at all.

Think about why many of these inmates have attitudes and are always ready to curse someone out. Every morning, they wake up to bars on the windows. They have to be told when to eat, when to sleep, and when to use the bathroom. Every day of their life is dictated by officers. So, how much more punishment do you want to give them? They are already separated from friends and family—and some have no one to put money on their books. I've watched so many of these men go hungry because they couldn't go to the chow hall due to officers abusing their authority. Every day that I was there, I understood more and more why God sent me there.

If the people I trained didn't learn anything else from me, they at least gained a better understanding of how to treat the inmates. Many of them told me that my advice made their job easier. But when I found out that sergeants wanted new officers to conform to harsh punishments, I knew I had a decision to make.

When I was told—indirectly—that I needed to start handing out tougher punishments if I wanted a promotion, I responded directly:

"Before I ever compromise my morals for a promotion, I will walk off this job. I treat all people as people, no matter what."

So many of us conform to what the world wants.

We compromise our integrity and morals—not just for ourselves, but in our relationship with God.

So, I ask you:

- What else in your life are you compromising?
- What have you allowed to become your master?
- Are you a slave to money?
- To the approval of others?
- To the desire to be liked and accepted?

Baby, I will walk away if the shoe doesn't fit.

I will NOT shrink my feet to fit the shoe. *Laugh out loud.*

Even though I was only there for five months, I learned how to expand my understanding—to see beyond just my perception and into others' perspectives. This is important for growth. Everyone is at different levels, and that's okay. If we are made in God's image, and God meets us where we are, then why don't we do the same for others?

I now understand why God sent me into that job.

Tyra Smith 51

It was never about a career—it was a test.

Before elevating me, God tested me:

- How would I treat His people?
- Would I abuse power and authority?
- Could I operate with empathy instead of control?

If I was going to write books on spiritual things, if I was going to step into leadership, then God needed to see if I was ready.

He does not take leadership lightly.

Especially now, in the times we are living in.

God is raising up leaders who:

- Won't compromise their integrity for money
- Won't conform just to fit in
- Aren't afraid to stand up and walk away from what isn't right
- Speak the truth with compassion

SHIFTED CONSCIOUSNESS

When I left this job in October, I knew what time it was. It was time to answer my second calling—writing.

This time, I didn't fight it. There was no need for God to pull me away and make me sit down to write. I willingly accepted the call.

The timing was no coincidence—I started my first book in October 2022, and exactly one year later, I started writing this book. We need to pay attention to the times and seasons when we tap into something new. That might be the very season God has chosen for you to create, move, or step into your purpose.

One day, God told me: "It is in darkness that we grow." Think about a seed—buried in the ground, surrounded by darkness. Yet in that darkness, it begins to grow. Just like a seed grows in darkness—so do we. Chaos comes to bring order. There are laws and principles to everything.

The Bible says, "So within, so without." This means: Whatever is in our inner world—our thoughts, emotions, and beliefs—creates our outer world. When we master the inner world, it will reflect in our outer reality. But it first starts within us.

For so long, I didn't realize that the battle inside me—especially around love—was affecting everything around me. It wasn't until I worked on healing myself that my reality began to change.

So, I ask you:

- What are you holding onto inside that is manifesting in your physical reality?
- If we are called to shift atmospheres, why wouldn't we also be called to shift our own consciousness?

Life is about the journey—not just the destination. If we focus only on the final destination, we miss the growth, the lessons, and the transformations along the way. I don't document my journey to expose people—but to help others free themselves from pain. By helping others, I heal myself too.

I have encountered:

- Betrayal
- Abuse
- Being used

But I now see that all of it was a setup for my comeback. We have to lose something to gain something better. Sometimes, we must be broken—mentally, emotionally, or physically. And that's okay. As long as you acknowledge the brokenness and trust that God is the ultimate fixer. Sometimes, we must break down before we rise again. So, don't be discouraged. Because you will rise.

ASCENSION

Quote by Tyra Smith